God's Shirt Pocket

Written and illustrated by

Emily Donels

Innovo Publishing

Published by
Innovo Publishing LLC
www.innovopublishing.com
1-888-546-2111

Innovo
Publishing

Providing Full-Service Publishing Services for
Christian Authors, Artists & Organizations: Hardbacks, Paperbacks,
eBooks, Audiobooks, Music & Videos.

GOD'S SHIRT POCKET

ISBN 13: 978-1-936076-42-0
ISBN 10: 1-936076-42-X

Cover Design & Interior Layout by Emily Donels and Innovo Publishing LLC

Printed in the United States of America
U.S. Printing History

First Edition: November 2010

Dedicated to my Heavenly Father
and to my Fabulous Five Encouragers:
Mom, Dad, my sister Missy, and my sisters by heart, Lisa & Liz

A special thanks to Terry Bailey and Innovo Publishing
for bringing *God's Shirt Pocket* to life!

It's a brand new day!

Ready for adventure,
I'm on my way.

Going out to discover,
explore, and see
just what's out there
waiting for me.

Jumping from rock to
rock while crossing
streams,

climbing mountains, going to all extremes.

Hiking to the top of the mountain,
above the trees so tall,
I take in the view and realize I am so small.

My Creator is bigger than anything I can see.
He made all these amazing things
with the same loving hands He made me!

Sitting down and resting my happy feet,

I imagine the soothing sound I hear
is the sound of God's heartbeat.

A sound as though I'm
reclining against His chest,
feeling loved and secure
as I take a rest.

Looking around and taking it all in,
    a thought comes to mind
            and I start to grin.

I know where I am. I
think I've got it.
Why, I must be in . . .

God's
Shirt
Pocket

My rest is over and out of His shirt pocket I go.
I grab my backpack;

there are still some trails below.

I make some twists and turns and end up going the wrong way. It is cold, empty, and dark. I have lost my way.

Then I cry out to God, "I've made a mess of it.

Please HELP me, Lord. I want out of this pit!"

Then up ahead I see a little glimmer of hope.

It takes a lot of hard work,
but I head up the slope.

HOPE

There is God with His arms reaching out,
waiting for me -- to help me, no doubt!

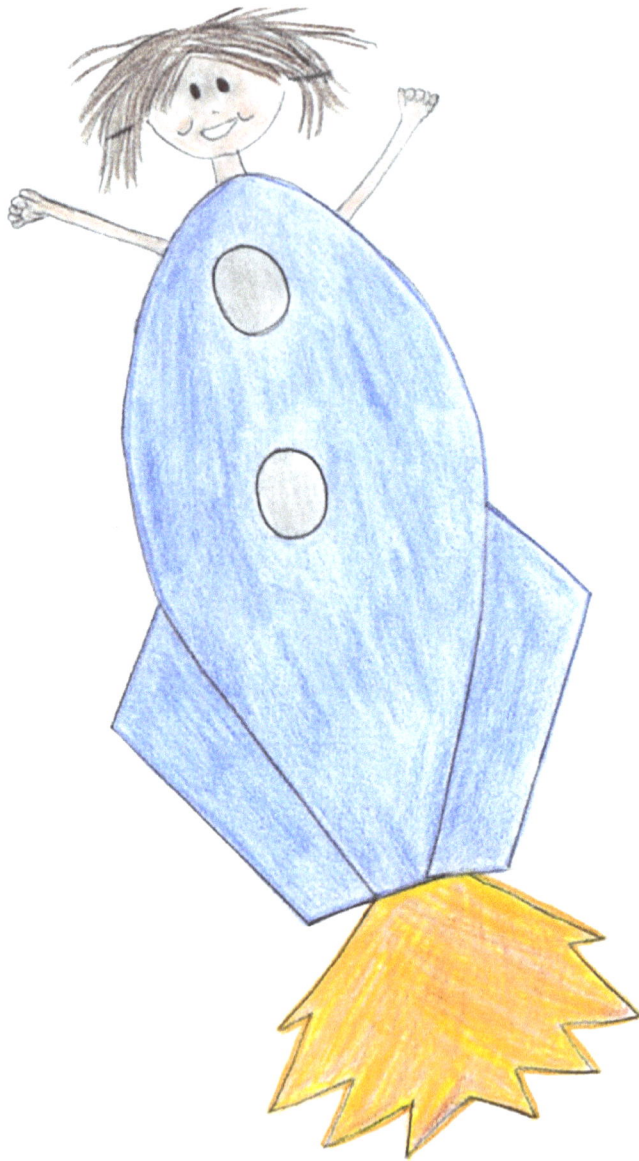

So eagerly I leap
forward,
as swift as a
soaring rocket,
to find safety
and security
inside of God's
shirt pocket.

And there again, that sweet, familiar sound . . .

the beating of His heart

calming me and turning it all around.

The comforting beat of His heart always reminds me
I'm safe, loved, and accepted and filled with complete JOY!

Yes, God holds me near to His heart,

never to remove His love, and He will never depart!

He treasures me as if I'm His favorite picture in His locket

while I walk with Him in His shirt pocket.

Walking with the Lord is an adventure;

and where I'm going next, I'm not always sure.

One thing I do know to be true:
when you walk with the Lord, He's always there for you.

"I'm Here"

"I'm Here"

Now there may be days I
climb out on my own

Tuesday

Saturday

feeling I don't need the Lord
and I can go alone.

Then I realize I'm not the same without His strength

Trust in the Lord   Proverbs 3:5
with all your heart
and lean not   on your
own understanding.

2nd

maybe for the 2nd time . . . or even the 10th !!

The lesson I continually learn along the way
is that my Savior is with me,
and He will guide me every day.

Today's Lesson:

+ = I'm not Alone

No better comfort will I ever find
than to rest in God's shirt pocket
and have peace of mind!

A Note from the Author

Hey, Friends,

I hope you've enjoyed this journey with me in *God's Shirt Pocket*. I love going on hiking adventures—seeing the mountains, waterfalls, leaves changing colors, and listening to the bubbling streams. Not only did God make all these beautiful things for us to enjoy but He also made us! And it doesn't stop there. God wants us to know Him personally. He is always with us, even when we make not-so-great choices.

Once when I was really sad, I kept reminding myself to read God's Word, to talk to Him, and to just imagine He was carrying me near His heart. My friend Lisa said, "Like you're in His shirt pocket!" That sweet thought, along with my love for hiking, helped me to understand what it looks like to walk with the Lord, and eventually it led me to write *God's Shirt Pocket*. My prayer is that you too will know the joy of walking closely with the Lord.

In Christ's Love,
Emily

www.ingramcontent.com/pod-product-compliance
Lightning Source LLC
Chambersburg PA
CBHW060819270326

41930CB00002B/92